SUGAR AND SPICE

CONGRATULATIONS
on securing your copy
of this book.

Left: The scene outside
W. H. Smith last year,
when supplies of the
previous book ran out.

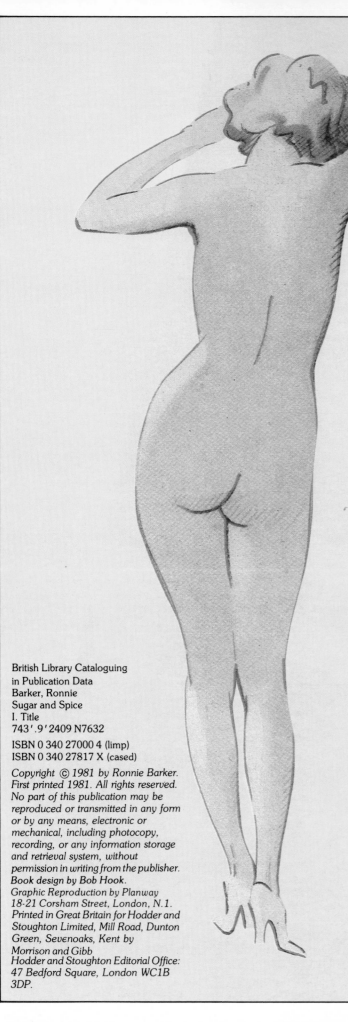

ACKNOWLEDGMENT

I would like, first, to acknowledge how deeply indebted I am to those brilliantly talented artists of the superb magazine, *La Vie Parisienne*, namely Messieurs Herouard, Guillaume, Mars, Vallet, Kirchner, Sahib, et les autres. Their work is unsurpassed in its verve and charm. I also am anxious to include all other artists, known and unknown, whose delightful ladies wander through these irreverent pages.

Secondly, I would like to thank the famous impresario, Mr Harold Fielding, for providing me with night work, leaving my days free to tackle the absorbing task of compiling this book.

Ronnie Barker

L'OEIL . . .

MADAME NARCISSE

British Library Cataloguing
in Publication Data
Barker, Ronnie
Sugar and Spice
I. Title
743′.9′2409 N7632

ISBN 0 340 27000 4 (limp)
ISBN 0 340 27817 X (cased)

*Book design by Bob Hook.
Graphic Reproduction by Planway
18-21 Corsham Street, London, N.1.
Printed in Great Britain for Hodder and
Stoughton Limited, Mill Road, Dunton
Green, Sevenoaks, Kent by
Morrison and Gibb
Hodder and Stoughton Editorial Office:
47 Bedford Square, London WC1B
3DP.*

Contents

LETTERS

POEMS
FEATURES
PLUS
PUZZLE
PAGES

"What are little girls made of? What are little girls made of?
Sugar and spice, and all things nice – that's what girls are made of!"
(NOW READ ON)

FOREWORD

The sugar and spice referred to in the title comes from the old nursery-rhyme, opposite, and can, I'm quite sure, taken to refer to big girls as well.

To all those who agree, as I do, with the simple sentiments contained in the verse, this book is dedicated. It is a picture book which sings a song of praise to the ladies: girls, women, call them what you will (and a lot of men do). This book, along with its two companion volumes *Sauce* and *Gentleman's Relish* is, I hope, a mirror, reflecting the ladies in all their moods, their fads, fashions, fancies, frills, foibles: domestic, social, sensual, and otherwise. To some, the mirror may appear a distorting one; others will acknowledge the fact that women come in all shapes and sizes. I, for one, am glad they do – and the seven hundred-odd pictures in these pages are certainly, to me, evidence enough.

The pictures – charming, comic, and occasionally sad, all, you will notice, depict an age gone by. A slower, perhaps less exciting, more leisurely time. Women were, we are told, much less free – the slaves, some would say, of marriage, of the kitchen, the bedroom, the factory, the servants' quarters.

I'm glad they no longer suffer. I'm all for free women (especially when nowadays everything else is so expensive); but I'm glad, also, to be able to leaf through these pages, and see how pretty they looked, in spite of it all!

How nice to watch them all cavorting by the seaside. How delightful to see them dressed for a fancy ball. And what a treat to get a good look at the servants' quarters!

We have only to turn the page.

Won't you join me?

Ronnie Barker

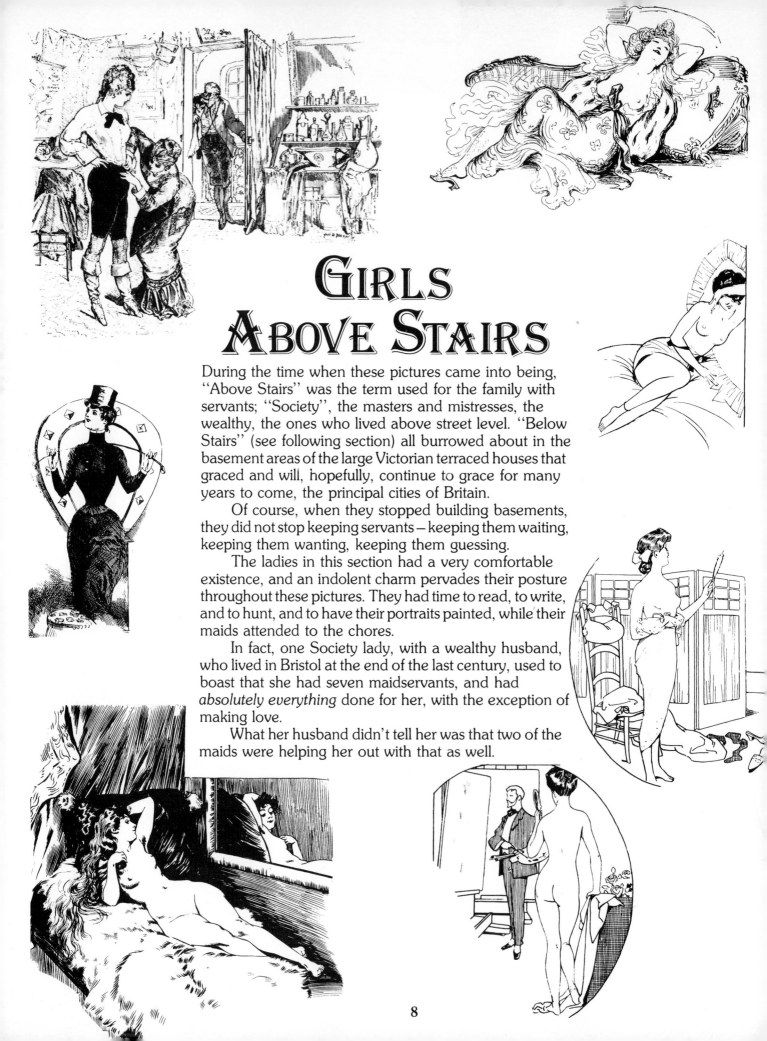

Girls Above Stairs

During the time when these pictures came into being, "Above Stairs" was the term used for the family with servants; "Society", the masters and mistresses, the wealthy, the ones who lived above street level. "Below Stairs" (see following section) all burrowed about in the basement areas of the large Victorian terraced houses that graced and will, hopefully, continue to grace for many years to come, the principal cities of Britain.

Of course, when they stopped building basements, they did not stop keeping servants – keeping them waiting, keeping them wanting, keeping them guessing.

The ladies in this section had a very comfortable existence, and an indolent charm pervades their posture throughout these pictures. They had time to read, to write, and to hunt, and to have their portraits painted, while their maids attended to the chores.

In fact, one Society lady, with a wealthy husband, who lived in Bristol at the end of the last century, used to boast that she had seven maidservants, and had *absolutely everything* done for her, with the exception of making love.

What her husband didn't tell her was that two of the maids were helping her out with that as well.

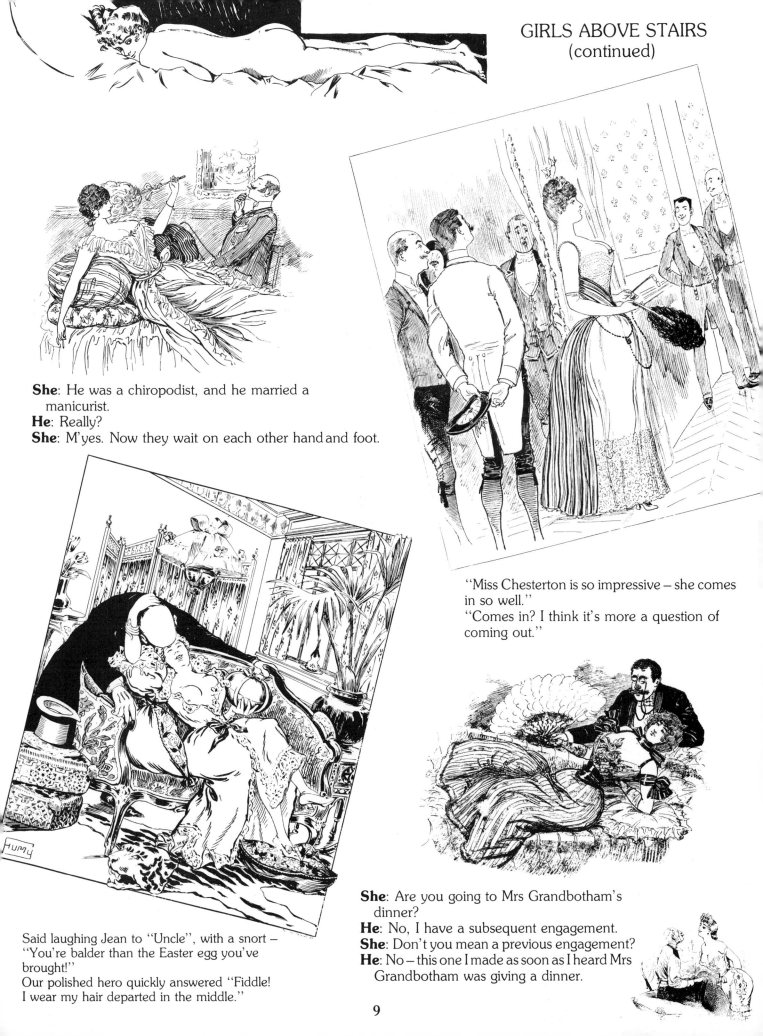

She: He was a chiropodist, and he married a
 manicurist.
He: Really?
She: M'yes. Now they wait on each other hand and foot.

"Miss Chesterton is so impressive – she comes
in so well."
"Comes in? I think it's more a question of
coming out."

Said laughing Jean to "Uncle", with a snort –
"You're balder than the Easter egg you've
brought!"
Our polished hero quickly answered "Fiddle!
I wear my hair departed in the middle."

She: Are you going to Mrs Grandbotham's
 dinner?
He: No, I have a subsequent engagement.
She: Don't you mean a previous engagement?
He: No – this one I made as soon as I heard Mrs
 Grandbotham was giving a dinner.

9

GIRLS ABOVE STAIRS
(continued)

The Honourable Ursula Flynn
Became so excessively thin,
That when she essayed
To drink lemonade,
She slipped through the straw
And fell in.

There was a young lady of Kent,
Whose nose was most awfully bent;
One morning she chose,
To follow her nose,
– And no one knew which way she went.

The girl who said when
she was married, she
would love her husband
for all he was worth.

She: That story about Lady Bumps is just
between us two.
Her: Oh well, between us two we should cover
quite a wide area.

"So. You're sending your wife away for a rest.
   Does she need one?"
"No, but I do!"

"Do you like cod-fish balls, Mr
   Smith?"
"I don't know. I've never been to
   one."

The Maid: It's ideal, Madam. Not only does it slim
   your waist, but it will stop you eating dinner.

I'm a result of a mixed
marriage. My father was a
man and my mother was a
woman.

It was Thursday, at eight, and they hadn't come late, yet the housemaid seemed
   puzzled and surly,
And their hosts were aghast, and untidy. Ah, yes. They'd turned up a week too early!

GIRLS ABOVE STAIRS (continued)

She: Your nose looks painted
He: Well it's not water-colour!

Old Boy: My wife treats me like a dog.
Young Thing: Well, she had you on a string
before you were married.

She: I'm looking for an ideal husband.
He: Oh really? Whose?

"Tell me, Lord Elpus, do you believe in clubs
for women?"
"Oh yes — but only if all other means of persuasion fail."

GIRLS ABOVE STAIRS (continued)

"Of course, there's a lot to be said in her favour,
but it's not nearly as interesting."

He: I've half a mind to enter Parliament.
She: Yes, that's all you need.

She: Is he a well-informed man?
He: I should think so. His wife tells him everything.

Young Ermintrude used all her
wiles, to earn her pile of plenty —
Not a man with a hundred
thousand pounds, but five
thousand men with twenty.

GIRLS ABOVE STAIRS (continued)

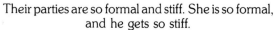

Their parties are so formal and stiff. She is so formal,
and he gets so stiff.

She: Oh dear.
What *does* one send a sick florist?

He: The doctor has given me just one month to live.
She: Good grief! Is it your wounds?
He: No my chauffeur. He used to drive for my
doctor.

The former Viceroy of Calcutta
Was cursed with a terrible stutter –
He screwed up his face
When he tried to say grace,
And he blew his false teeth in the butter.

GIRLS ABOVE STAIRS (continued)

He: I'm not in very good voice tonight.
She: Don't worry —
we've got no ear for music.

Mother: Whenever my daughter plays that French tune, you
weep. Are you French?
Man: No, I'm a musician.

"She really has an unusual voice. It's like asthma set to music."

I'm told Wagner's music is much better than it sounds.

At a party, why is it always the lady who can't sing who does?

I can't sing a note, but I get sent a lot of them.

She: It's lovely. Who wrote it?
He: Mozart.
She: And is he still composing?
He: No – unfortunately, he is decomposing.

GIRLS ABOVE STAIRS (continued)

PHYLLIS HOOTERS BALL

(to the tune of "Phil the Fluter's Ball")

Now you've heard of Phyllis Hooter
Of Hooterbury Hall
The day the darling came of age
Her father gave a ball.
The girls from all the county came
They curtsied and they cooed,
And we fellows sat and stared at all
That female pulchritude.

There was Jean, there was June,
There was Janet there was Jennifer
And Jane and Joyce and Jacqueline
And Juliet and Joan.
There was Lily who was silly
There was Bessy who was messy
There was Annie with her grannie
And Fanny on her own.

And they all stood round, looking
  rather ineffectual
Their feet close together and their
  bottoms to the wall.
And some were dim, and others
  intellectual
And some were fairly sexual, and
  others weren't at all.

There was Claire, there was Chris
There was Connie and Clarissa
And Cecilia and Charity and Caroline
  and Kate.
There was shrinking little Violet
Who doesn't want to marry yet
And bulging little Harriet
Who can't afford to wait.

Now, Clarissa you could kiss her
You could meddle with Nerissa and
Vanessa you could press her and
Caress against the wall.
You could *have* fun with Nicola
But if you tried to tickle her
You'd end up with Virginia
Who wouldn't do at all.

There was Cora, Dora, Norah, Thora,
Flora and Felicity
Their sweetness and simplicity
Enchanted one and all.
Though I yearned for *every* one of 'em
I finished up with none of 'em –
I went home on my ownsome from
Phyllis Hooter's Ball!

GIRLS BELOW STAIRS

"Below Stairs", in contrast to the previous section, was a never-ending round of work and toil from considerably before sunrise until well after dark.

Always at the wrong end of the bell-rope or speaking-tube, the poor girls were rushed off their feet by their mistresses, and often persuaded off them by their masters.

But the girls herein seem to be surviving – for the most part they are a cheery and a saucy-looking lot, and I hope you will appreciate their efforts to please as much as I do.

ROAST BEEF OF OLD EN[...]

The new maid:
The Bible says man is made of dust. If that's true, there would soon have been one under the carpet.

He: How's the new maid?
She: Oh, she's like a blotter. She soaks it all in, and gets it all backwards.

The Master: That flour you bought last week was very tough, Janet. My wife made some biscuits and we couldn't eat them.

"I can lie in bed in the morning, and watch the sun rise."
"That's nothing. I can sit in the scullery and see the kitchen sink."

"That's twice you've forgotten to add the lard."
"I know. It's so greasy it slips my memory."

He: I'm not rich, I don't own a château, or a big car, like Alphonse Leclerc, but I love you, Michelle, and want to marry you.
She: I love you too, dear – but tell me more about Alphonse Leclerc.

Lady Hairdresser: Excuse me, you dropped your toupee.

I'd love a Mediterranean cruise, and a sable coat,
and some velvet shoes,

I'd love a couple of million dollars, and some silk night-gowns with real lace collars,

I'd like a nip of spring in the air, and a brand new face, and coal-black hair —

But most of all, a convincing cough, that will get me Monday and Tuesday off.

One for the governor.

Mistress: I thought I heard a young man's voice in this bedroom earlier. Were you entertaining?
Maid: That's for him to say, Madam.

Some domestic legs —
and the feet they are
usually rushed off.

Barmaid: I used to be in service, but they
didn't keep a cat or a dog, so there was
no one to blame for breakages.

Mistress: . . . and furthermore, Agnes, I would be obliged if you did not argue with me.

Agnes: I didn't say a word.

Mistress: Well, you were listening in a very aggressive manner.

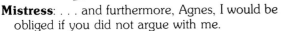

Old One: They're so highbrow! Every time they have a row, they keep me running between the keyhole and the dictionary!

The master started off by calling this girl "Sugar", and ended up by paying her a lump sum.

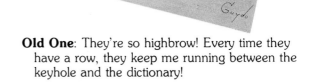

Mistress: Mr Jones and I are retiring now, Maud.

Maud the Maid: Very well, Madam. When would you like to be woken up?

Mistress: We'll ring when we want to be woken up, thank you.

Manservant (helpfully): My previous employer used to say that when your income is exceeded by your outgo, then your upkeep is your downfall, and the outcome of the income depends on the outgo for the upkeep, Sir.

GIRLS BELOW STAIRS (continued)

"I'd like to take out one of the children, Elsie. Bring
me one that matches my dress, would you?"

"Don't let the sun into the drawing-room, Clara, it
might fade the goldfish."

Mistress: I saw the milkman kissing you this
morning, Joan. In future, I will take the milk in.
Maid: It's no use, Madam. He's promised to kiss
nobody but me.

Maid: This lady says she has called about a
contribution to the home for inebriates, Madam.
Mistress: Oh, good. She can have my husband.

Master (to maid, who has never posed before):
    What do you think of it, Belinda?
Maid: Well, I think the expression is very good.

GIRLS BELOW STAIRS (continued)

"ENJOYING MY NEW POSITION"...

A few of the kind of postcards sent between the
girls below stairs in Edwardian days; and some of
the girls who might have sent them.

GIRLS BELOW STAIRS (continued)

Here, straight from the pages of *La Vie Parisienne* during the Naughty Nineties, are some joyfully stylish drawings of our early ancestors, above and below stairs. The French words are intact. Those of you who read French may have the added pleasure of the writers' witty text.* I have not inserted subtitles; the pictures speak for themselves.

*(AUTHOR'S NOTE: As I do not read French well enough to understand the captions, they may be terribly dull for all I know. I hope they're not rude. I should really have got someone to interpret them for me. Perhaps I had better *see* if . . . too late now. Oh dear. Stammer, mumble, stumble, crash. Exit.)

GRÈCE ANTIQUE
LA TOILETTE

On le sait, elles avaient le culte de leur beauté et de leur corps, leurs seins étaient l'objet d'attentions multiples : ils étaient lustrés avec de la nacre réduite en poudre très fine et assimilée à une huile odorante. Une bandelette de cuir souple, premier vestige du corset, les soutenait, posée à même la peau. En l'attachant, pense sans doute « aux beaux jeunes gens qui mettront à sa porte, le matin, des vers avec des guirlandes de roses »

Faisait ses ablutions très complètes à l'eau froide, puis « une éponge plongée dans une jarre d'huile de senteur venait caresser son corps, avant de le frotter avec une étoffe rugueuse qui fit rougir sa peau assouplie », pour corriger la dureté que l'emploi de l'eau froide eût donnée à l'épiderme. Écoute religieusement « l'esclave qui depuis sept ans lui enseigne jusqu'aux derniers détails l'art complexe et voluptueux des grandes courtisanes ».

Sa toison de cheveux, blonds par l'usage constant d'eau de chaux ou de teintures déjà savantes, était soigneusement lavée et parfumée comme le reste du corps, et les fards jouaient un grand rôle dans la mise en valeur de sa beauté. Du noir aux cils, sourcils, paupières ; du rose aux ongles, aux coudes, aux pommettes ; du bleu aux veines. Avec un pinceau, une esclave dessinait à sa taille les trois plis de Vénus et simulait deux fossettes dans sa croupe arrondie.

Assise dans un siège de marbre, sa chevelure est édifiée en coiffures variées, depuis le *Corqubus*, coiffure des dames d'Athènes, ou l'*Anodima*, bandeau orné, pour soutenir les cheveux et les trois bandelettes de soie, les épingles d'or que la statuaire a immortalisées. Choisit les sandales nouées de lanières qu'elle portera, les bracelets, les bagues, les colliers dont elle se parera, la pièce de lin rose ou jaune dont elle s'enveloppera, et l'éventail de plumes, et les boucles d'agate qui la rafraîchiront, si son caprice ne lui fait rechercher le contact froid d'un petit serpent sur sa blanche poitrine.

Portait un seul vêtement intime, petite chemise de toile très fine, courte, étroite, sans manches, ne dépassant pas le gras de la cuisse. Revêtait ensuite une simple tunique retenue sur l'épaule par des camées. Laïs et Phryné furent aimées ainsi.

A. Vignota

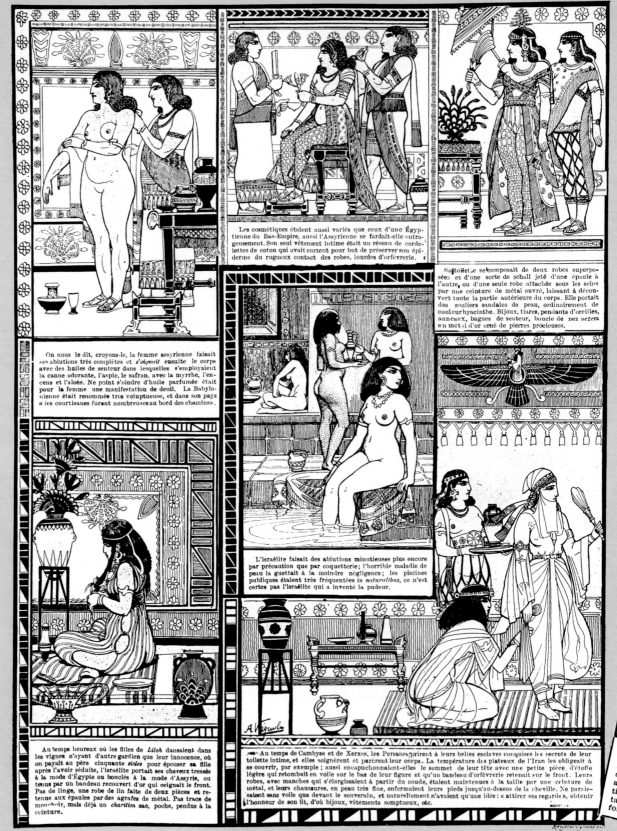

Les cosmétiques étaient aussi variés que ceux d'une Égyptienne du Bas-Empire, aussi l'Assyrienne se fardait-elle outrageusement. Son seul vêtement intime était un réseau de cordelettes de coton qui avait surtout pour but de préserver son épiderme du rugueux contact des robes, lourdes d'orfèvrerie.

On nous le dit, croyons-le, la femme assyrienne faisait ses ablutions très complètes et s'oignait ensuite le corps avec des huiles de senteur dans lesquelles s'employaient la canne odorante, l'aspic, le safran, avec la myrrhe, l'encens et l'aloès. Ne point s'oindre d'huile parfumée était pour la femme une manifestation de deuil. La Babylonienne était renommée très voluptueuse, et dans son pays « les courtisanes furent nombreuses au bord des chemins ».

Sa toilette se composait de deux robes superposées et d'une sorte de schall jeté d'une épaule à l'autre, ou d'une seule robe attachée sous les seins par une ceinture de métal ouvré, laissant à découvert toute la partie antérieure du corps. Elle portait des souliers sandales de peau, ordinairement de couleur hyacinthe. Bijoux, tiares, pendants d'oreilles, anneaux, bagues de senteur, boucle de nez nezem en métal d'or orné de pierres précieuses.

L'israélite faisait des ablutions minutieuses plus encore par précaution que par coquetterie; l'horrible maladie de peau la guettait à la moindre négligence; les piscines publiques étaient très fréquentées in naturalibus, ce n'est certes pas l'israélite qui a inventé la pudeur.

Au temps heureux où les filles de Liloh dansaient dans les vignes n'ayant d'autre gardien que leur innocence, où on payait au père cinquante sicles pour épouser sa fille après l'avoir séduite, l'israélite portait ses cheveux tressés à la mode d'Égypte ou bouclés à la mode d'Assyrie, ou tenus par un bandeau recouvert d'or qui ceignait le front. Pas de linge, une robe de lin faite de deux pièces et retenue aux épaules par des agrafes de métal. Pas trace de mouchoir, mais déjà un charitim sac, poche, pendus à la ceinture.

Au temps de Cambyse et de Xerxès, les Persanes prirent à leurs belles esclaves conquises les secrets de leur toilette intime, et elles soignèrent et parèrent leur corps. La température des plateaux de l'Iran les obligeait à se couvrir, par exemple; aussi encapuchonnaient-elles le sommet de leur tête avec une petite pièce d'étoffe légère qui retombait en voile sur le bas de leur figure et qu'un bandeau d'orfèvrerie retenait sur le front. Leurs robes, avec manches qui s'élargissaient à partir du coude, étaient maintenues à la taille par une ceinture de métal, et leurs chaussures, en peau très fine, enfermaient leurs pieds jusqu'au-dessus de la cheville. Ne paraissaient sans voile que devant le souverain, et naturellement n'avaient qu'une idée: « attirer ses regards », obtenir l'honneur de son lit, d'où bijoux, vêtements somptueux, etc.

Ablutions
raffinements
ferment du
dile, pour b
apprêté en p
tiques donnen
tante, mais il
fondrait.

La femme gauloise prenait autant de soin de son corps que la femme grecque ou romaine. L'usage antique du tatouage existait encore à l'époque de la conquête, mais elle ne se teignait plus le corps avec une couleur bleue extraite du pastel ; elle lavait son visage avec de l'écume de bière, se fardait avec du vermillon sur ses joues et se teignait les sourcils avec de la craie dissoute dans du vinaigre, était du vermillon sur ses joues et se teignait les sourcils avec de la suie ou avec un liquide tiré de l'orphe, un poisson très commun sur les côtes de Bretagne.

La femme romaine employait aussi « des poudres astringentes pour réprimer la transpiration ; une pommade de pâte de fèves pour teindre la peau et en effacer les rides, une autre appelée *psilotrum*, qui est un remède épilatoire ; des pastilles de myrte et de lentisques pétries avec du vin vieux et des taies de lierre et de myrrhe pour parfumer l'haleine ».

Sous la domination romaine, les Gauloises riches adoptent les modes de Rome. « Elles soutiennent leurs seins avec un corset appelé *strophium*, elles se coiffent à la romaine, portent la chemise courte et une robe très longue appelée *stolla* : leur goût pour les bijoux est qualifié d'immodéré, leur goût des beaux hommes également.

Les artifices étaient déjà pratiqués : légers coussins pour dissimuler l'inégalité d'une taille, larges bandelettes de cuir de bœuf pour comprimer un sein trop fort. Et « le goût effréné du luxe s'empara des dames romaines, le vieux Caton dénonça le fléau ». On comptait jusqu'à dix-huit sortes de robes et de manteaux, la *regilla*, la *mendicule*, l'*impluviata*, la tunique *spissa*, le *pluma-tile*, le *laconicum*, etc.

Leurs belles chevelures, rougies par l'usage constant de l'eau de chaux, flottaient le plus souvent libres sous une espèce de cercle ; après l'invasion, les Gauloises adoptèrent les coiffures grecques et romaines, le *corymbus*, l'*anadema*, bandeau orné mis en arrière, le *diadema* des déesses et des grandes dames. Le plus souvent, leurs cheveux étaient poudrés avec des cendres blanches, finement tamisées.

parfums, la Romaine use de tous les
elle, des petits vases d'albâtre ren-
niment tiré des excréments du croco-
peau ; du céruse, résidu de plomb,
on fait venir de Rhodes. Ces cosmé-
maine un teint d'une blancheur écla-
e évite le soleil, autrement ce teint

Avant que le bas ne fît son apparition, vers le temps d'Auguste, paraît-il, la Romaine portait des chaussettes, un caleçon d'un tissu délicat, et sa chemise se composait d'une pièce d'étoffe fendue par le milieu pour passer la tête et dont l'arrière et l'avant se reliaient par deux broches. Ce fut la *palla succincta*. Ses cheveux étaient enveloppés quelquefois d'un réseau d'or, ou bien on y enlaçait des bandelettes, on encore on leur donnait la forme d'un cimier. Elle portait des souliers de peau blanche ou des thurnes de pourpre, « charmant ornement d'un pied mignon ».

A. Vignola

Women on the Town
(AND OF THE TOWN)

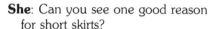

This section could be said to be all-embracing, and although the same cannot *necessarily* be said of the girls included in it, nevertheless they are a much more social, even friendly, bunch.

In the case of the ladies *of* the town, it is their job to be friendly – and the girls who adorn the following pages are certainly that. They do not wait to be approached. They approach you, offering their services as escorts, on the town. Some make a small charge; others move more slowly.

Of course, the ladies in this section are not only girls of the streets; some are simply girls *in* the street, paying more attention to their umbrellas than their skirts in the windy weather. But, whatever their occupations or preoccupations, the artists have given their creations a liveliness which is a joy to behold.

She: Can you see one good reason for short skirts?
He: I can see two of them.

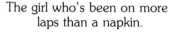

The girl who's been on more laps than a napkin.

DINNER ON THE STAIRS
(or seduction,
step by step)

The Earl: Married? No, my dear. Women are like elephants —
nice to look at, but you wouldn't want to own one.

It isn't usually the cold girls that get the fur coats . . .

How daintily, how prettily, this
sweet girl passes by,
With the spike on that umbrella she
is bound to catch your eye.

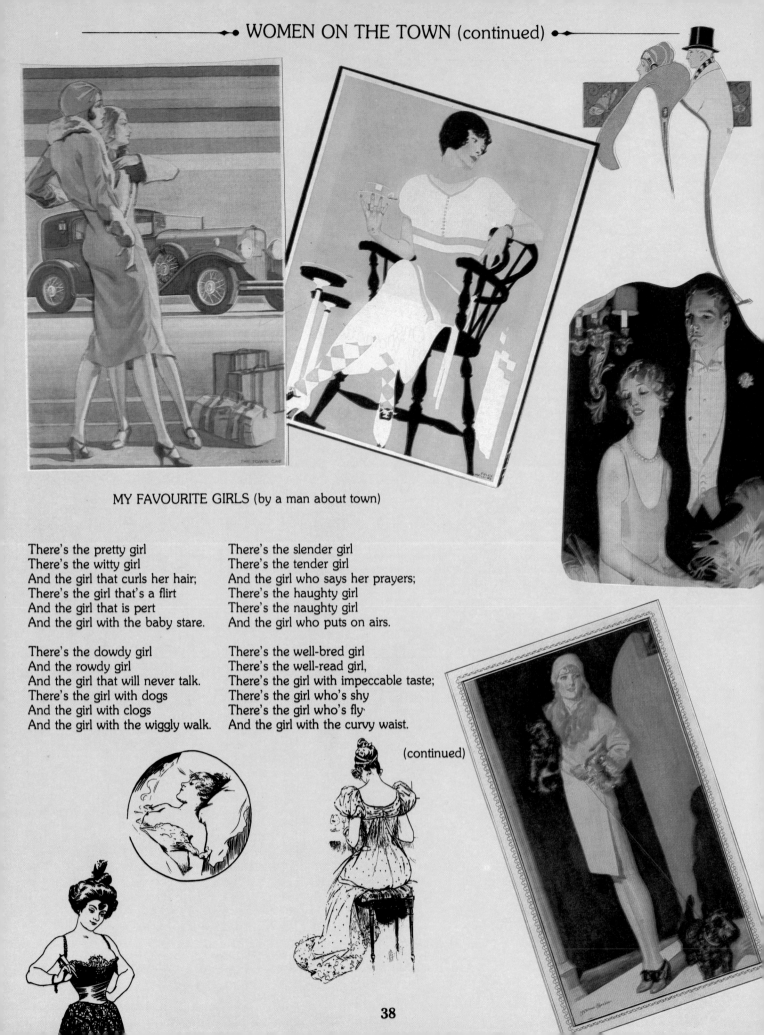

MY FAVOURITE GIRLS (by a man about town)

There's the pretty girl
There's the witty girl
And the girl that curls her hair;
There's the girl that's a flirt
And the girl that is pert
And the girl with the baby stare.

There's the dowdy girl
And the rowdy girl
And the girl that will never talk.
There's the girl with dogs
And the girl with clogs
And the girl with the wiggly walk.

There's the slender girl
There's the tender girl
And the girl who says her prayers;
There's the haughty girl
There's the naughty girl
And the girl who puts on airs.

There's the well-bred girl
There's the well-read girl,
There's the girl with impeccable taste;
There's the girl who's shy
There's the girl who's fly
And the girl with the curvy waist.

(continued)

MY FAVOURITE GIRLS (continued)

So I'll drink to the girl with a face that is fair
To the girl with the figure that's wavy;
I'll drink with the girl with the delicate air
Who drinks with the Army and Navy;
I'll drink to the girl who has breeding and
    gold,
I'll drink below stairs, with the slavey;
But I'll *marry* the girl who is both rich and old —
The girl with one foot in the gravy.

WOMEN ON THE TOWN (continued)

He: I can stay awake any length of time by just forcing myself to do it.
She: I see – a triumph of mind over mattress; or is it mistress?

Mary had a little lamb,
Its fleece was white as snow,
And everywhere that Mary went,
The lamb was sure to go.

Mary went to London town
And met some Soho waiters,
Mary had a little lamb,
Some peas, and some potatoes.

She: The Rent? Oh, could you call again? As you see, I'm just going out.

She wears the frills and
fripperies
Of a girl of the
Demi-Monde,
But wears black garters in
memory
Of those who've gone
beyond.

She: What a terrible figure she has! I've seen better legs on a kitchen table.

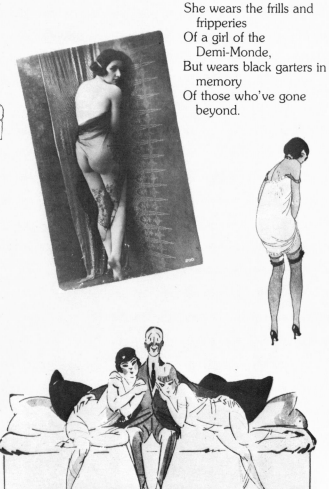

He: Would you live with a man who had a million pounds?
She: Of course – I would be a fool not to.
He: And would you live with the same man if he had five pounds?
She: Of course I wouldn't – what kind of woman do you think I am?
He: We've just established the *kind* of woman you are. What we are doing now is haggling over the price.

She: He has his two feet planted firmly on the ground.
Her: That's very nice, but how does he get his trousers off?

WOMEN
ON THE TOWN
(continued)

The Same Poem . . .

A ROMANTIC'S VIEW

Gold is the colour of my true love's hair
As she raises up her glass
And the candle shines through the wine's red
   glow,
And the evenings gently pass.

Green is the colour of my true love's eyes,
Eyes that I can't resist,
They glow through the smoke of her cigarette
Like Jade through the morning mist.

from two points of view.

A REALIST'S VIEW

Red is the colour of a June-bloomed rose
When plucked from its briar's posy –
But red is the colour of my true love's nose
When she's been at the Rouge or the Rosé.

Yellow is the colour of the dawning sun
That creeps where the frost still lingers,
But yellow is the colour of my true love's
   thumb,
And brown is the colour of her fingers.

WOMEN ON THE TOWN (continued)

She: Ah, Mr Ponsonby, I've been expecting you – if it *is* you.
How nice to see you, except that I can't.
Are you him, or isn't it you?

She: I'm too tall for you. I'm six foot two with my hat on.
He: I'm seven foot nine with my umbrella up.

She: I never knew what real happiness was until I got married.
He: Yes, Madam, I know – but by then it's too late.

He: Too décolleté? I don't think so. I went out to dinner last night with a girl whose dress was cut so low that I had to look under the table to see what she was wearing.

She: You seemed very friendly with that woman. How do you know her?
He: Now, dear. I met her professionally.
She: Whose profession? Yours or hers?

She: Water attracts electricity.
He: Have you tested that theory?
She: Yes, every time I get into the bath the telephone rings.

The romantic one: . . . and at the end of his letter he put two X's. What does that mean?
The cynic: It means he's double-crossing you.

She: We met; it blossomed into friendship; it ripened into love; then it rotted into marriage.

WOMEN ON THE TOWN (concluded)

Making Hay

Mother Nature

"Country girls are pretty, you ought to see them dance – they kick their legs above their heads, and show their Sunday pants" was what we used to chant, as children, in some skipping game or other.

I don't think they do. I think it's a fantasy, as indeed are many of the characteristics and habits attributed to country girls.

A few pages only here, and, without doubt, all fantasy – from the golden and muscular god of summer sprinkling his largesse over the countryside, down to the city gent popping out from behind the scarecrow, and surprising the peasant girl by the river.

I don't think it really goes on, do you? But it is nice to imagine it might do, somewhere . . .

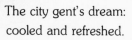

The city gent's dream:
cooled and refreshed.

An awful lot of bull.

The Flowers
of the Field

She: I'm a wood-nymph.
He: Oh – well I wood, if you wood.

The flowers of field, when you see them picked and
    peeled
Are so pretty that you can't forget-me-not 'em;
There's Lily and Fritillary, Geranium and Rose,
And dear little pink Apple-bottom.

45

WOMEN IN THE COUNTRY (continued)

People get tired of living in town
They move to the country and all settle down
They build themselves houses and roads, and then
They all have to move to the country again.

Scarecrow Gent: I'm sorry to trouble you, but according to my guide-book, there should be a public house near here.
Water-Sprite: Ar, that's what moi Dad be always saying.

"It's all right – take your clothes off. No one will see you."
"Hardly worth taking them off then, is it?"

He: Are all the girls in the village as beautiful as you?
She: I don't know – I only look at the boys.

He used to call for me every day but now he's got that car,
Sometimes he comes, sometimes he don't – I don't know
  where I are.
Now he's gone all mechanical, *my* charms are not enough –
He whizzes round like a vacuum cleaner, picking up bits of
  fluff.

Farmer: Married, Sir? Of course you are. I knew that
straight away – your missus be wearing the trousers!

"You say your father
makes his living by the pen?"
"Yessir – he keeps chickens."

The girl by the stile has been waiting awhile, for the boy with the dog to
  appear,
Each Sunday at eight she goes there to wait, and has done for over a year.
Up to now he has always been there, never missed, and I don't think I
  blame him, do you?
With a girl like that waiting, for you, to be kissed, on the stile she's
  accustomed to?

WHERE ARE THEY ALL GOING?

THEY ARE ALL
GOING TO THE NEXT PAGE,

TO SAMPLE THE
BRIGHT AND
BREEZY
DELIGHTS OF . . .

GIRLS AT THE SEASIDE

A SCRAP-BOOK

GIRLS AT THE SEASIDE (continued)

There is nowhere quite like the seaside for bringing out the most sugarful and spice-ridden in the ladies. They go there to get brown, they go there to relax; they go there for exercise, for romance. But chiefly, they go there to be looked at.

And you won't get many men looking the other way when a pair of bronzed cheeks go by – whichever direction they are walking.

Mary: Would you care if he left you?
Mirabel: Not if he left me enough.

She: Why is it that women learn to swim easier than men?
He: Simple. No one wants to teach men.

Unfair camouflage!

He: My! Just think how she must look in a bathing suit.

She: It can't be much of a yacht – he says he keeps it in a basin.

52

"A girl's face may be her fortune, but it's the other parts that draw interest."

"A girl can either go to the lakes and see the scenery, or go to the seaside and be the scenery."

Young Jones took the Smythe twins (both beautiful girls),
To the seashore, and then to a show;
Then to supper as well, then a three-star hotel –
Was it worth it? we ask. Yes and no.

He: Did you call for help?
She: Yes – but you're not the man.

She: I don't go out with strange men.
He: You've known me all your life.
She: I still think you're strange.

She: It seems there are no married men here this summer.
Her: There must be. There are ten men at the hotel and I've only had nine proposals.

"Imagination . . . that fills out ends of memory,
Like sails upon the wind." (Longfellow)

Seven surfing sisters, stayed out very
  late,
One slipped up stupidly, and then
  there were eight.

Pearl fishing underwater.
Pearls are delightful things to get hold of, as you can
  see.
(The girl in the boat is her sister.)

55

One girl (to the other): He told me his wife didn't mind a scrap if he took our photograph.
The other: No – in fact I think she's enjoying it.

Young Elsie was a timid child – but not so, now she's older;
There's lots of pebbles on the beach, but she's a little boulder.

A girl who's the picture of health, must look after her frame . . .

Watch out for sunburn.

I went for a walk with Dulcie
She went for a walk with me
We went for a walk by the briny,
Down by the shiny sea.
The wind blew up our under-drawers
As lively as could be,
The wind blew both our hats off
So we both went home to tea.

"Two Scotsmen on the beach yesterday each bet the
other a pound that they could stay under water longest."
"What happened?"
"They both drowned."

57

She: I have the body of a girl of twenty.
He: You'd better give it back – you're stretching it.

"I want to be seen in all the best places."
"Why not join a nudist colony?"

—— THE SIREN ——

Hiding behind my parasol, my tell-tale tail unwound,
Trying to lure a mortal man – I lie on the sandy ground.
He's been there for an hour or more; I wonder, would he be around
If he knew my statistics were 38, 24 and 3 shillings a pound?

"So you told Charlie you loved him after all?"
"I didn't want to, but he squeezed it out of me."

"That reminds I, Martha,
it be full moon tonight."

I'd caught nothing all day
When I heard someone say
"Dispense with your clothes,
and be bold!"

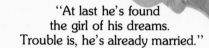

And to my surprise
I caught several eyes
And a winkle or two, and a cold.

"At last he's found
the girl of his dreams.
Trouble is, he's already married."

"This costume is so embarrassing, I daren't
show my face!"

He: Am I the first man you ever kissed?
She: It's possible. Were you in Eastbourne
six years ago?

Short-sighted gent: Look out, George, there's some pretty hefty-looking rocks over there.

He's a perfect gentleman, but I think it's better than no boyfriend at all.

ADVT: Girl, willing to take the plunge with the right man, with no strings attached.
(Cupids Weekly Messenger)

Women
AT HOME

A woman's place is in the home. But who originally said so? Certainly not a woman, from my experience. She usually can't wait to get out of it. No, it must have been a married man – the same man who, before he married her, used to lie awake all night, thinking about something she had said – and who now falls asleep before she has finished saying it.

Nevertheless, the home is where you'll find most women – while their husbands are out earning the daily bread, they are at home, cutting the crusts off it and making it into a bread-and-butter pudding.

These next pages, then, are devoted to pictures of the ladies in their natural habitat. As pretty as ever, as comic as usual, as delightful as always.

Women's Liberation protestation, however, is kept to a minimum here. We hear, and have heard, sufficient elsewhere for the next hour or two. For although women have been misjudged and mistreated in a thousand ways, there is one way in which they have never suffered. They have never suffered in silence.

Because, generally speaking, women are generally speaking. Mind you, a woman doesn't always get the last word; sometimes she is speaking to another woman!

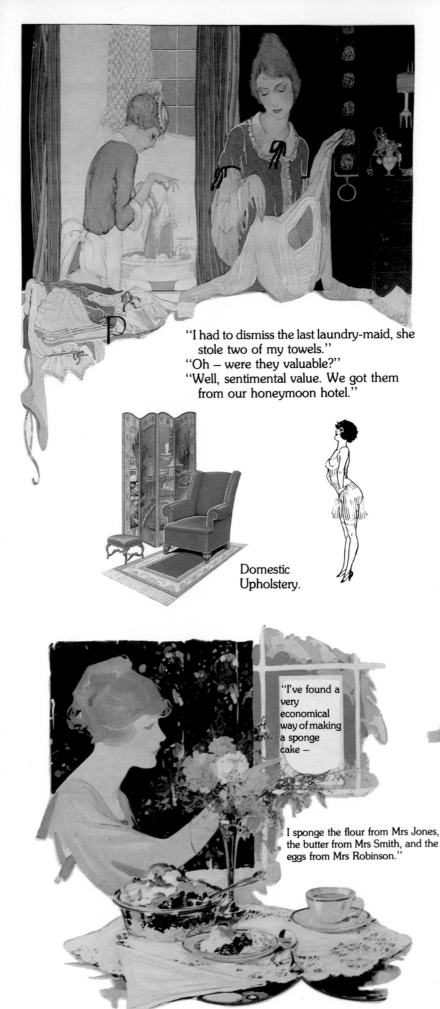

"I had to dismiss the last laundry-maid, she stole two of my towels."
"Oh – were they valuable?"
"Well, sentimental value. We got them from our honeymoon hotel."

Domestic Upholstery.

"I've found a very economical way of making a sponge cake –

I sponge the flour from Mrs Jones, the butter from Mrs Smith, and the eggs from Mrs Robinson."

The Pink One: They say marriage is like a warm bath.
The Yellow One: Yes – once you get used to it, it's not so hot.

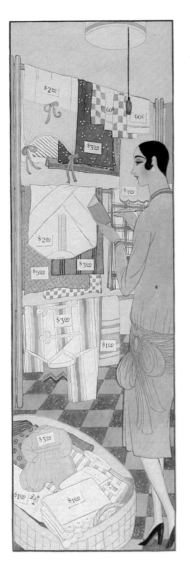

Freedom

I buy all his shirts, I select all his ties,
And I pick out his underpants, too;
And he always remarks "What a lovely surprise!
You clever old thing, they are just the right size."
And he tenderly smiles with those tired spaniel
    eyes,
And I do wish he wouldn't, I do, I do,
I do wish he wouldn't, I do.

I wash all his shirts and I iron them all flat
And I see that they're aired through and through;
When he leaves for the office I hand him his hat
He says "See you at tea, and we'll have a nice
    chat,"
Gives my cheek a quick kiss, and my bottom a
    pat,
And I do wish he didn't, I do, I do,
I do wish he didn't, I do.

For I long to be free of this prison called home
And the road to the North calls my name –
For my folk were all fishers, and followed the
    foam,
And this city life's turgid and tame.

But I clean all the house and I dust and I shine
And I talk it all over with Pru,
With painted-on smiles we pretend life is gay,
And of course married life is the only real way,
And I think how he loves me so much, and I pray
Oh I pray that he didn't, I do, I do,
Oh I pray that he didn't, I do.

He: I was talking to the caretaker yesterday. The idiot told me that he had made love to every woman in this building, except one. Can you believe that?
She: Yes. I bet it's that stuck-up Mrs Johnson on the ground floor.

She (wearing her new dress): But look at it this way, my dear – The dress was originally marked a hundred pounds – but it was reduced to fifty. So I saved fifty pounds – and that's the fifty pounds I bought the dress with, you see?

She: I was a silly goose when I married you.
He: Well you were certainly no chicken.

He: More money? Good gracious, where does all the money I give you for food get to?
She: Just stand sideways and look in the mirror!

A few differences of Opinion . . .

A woman who talks all day
Deserves a husband who
snores all night.

She: I cook and bake for you and what do I get?
Nothing!
He: You're lucky. I get indigestion.

Marriage was made in Heaven . . .

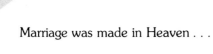

but then, so were
Thunder and
Lightning . . .

65

Housework for the Sporting Girl

A practical way of
combining training
with her daily chores.

The
HIGH-JUMPER

The
SKATER

The
GYMNAST

The
TENNIS PLAYER

The
BIG-GAME HUNTER

My Favourite Room

The kitchen's my favourite venue,
Especially when love's on the
  menu –
When the day's at an end,
It's so nice, with a friend,
To share some warm tit-bits
  between you.

My favourite's the room that you sit
  in –
It's a room you can nod off or knit in;
And if boys do get rough
The sofa's quite tough,
And the chairs you can do quite a bit
  in.

My favourite's the
  one with the bath,
Where I lie like a cat
  on a hearth,
Soaked in suds for
  an hour
Then it's into the
  shower
To experience a cold
  aftermath.

My favourite room is the loo,
I think it's so private, don't you?
It's the finest place known
To sit on your own
When you find you've got not
  much to do.

My favourite's the one with the bed in
  it,

Oh, the dangerous words that are said
  in it!
Oh, the promises made!
Oh, the parts that are played!
(But I prefer sleeping instead in it.)

WHAT THEY WEAR UNDERNEATH

The corset advertisements of the twenties' magazines were no different from all the others, before or since; that is, they all contain pictures of girls who would never need a corset in the first place. Or, in fact, in any place. These slim, willowy reeds waft around in glove-like garments which give the appearance of having been upholstered, or even, in some cases, soled and heeled (see opposite).

How different from the comic-postcard reality of a creaking, straining, press-stud-popping thing of shiny pink, about to burst in all directions . . .

"THE LOST C(H)ORD"

WHAT THEY WEAR UNDERNEATH

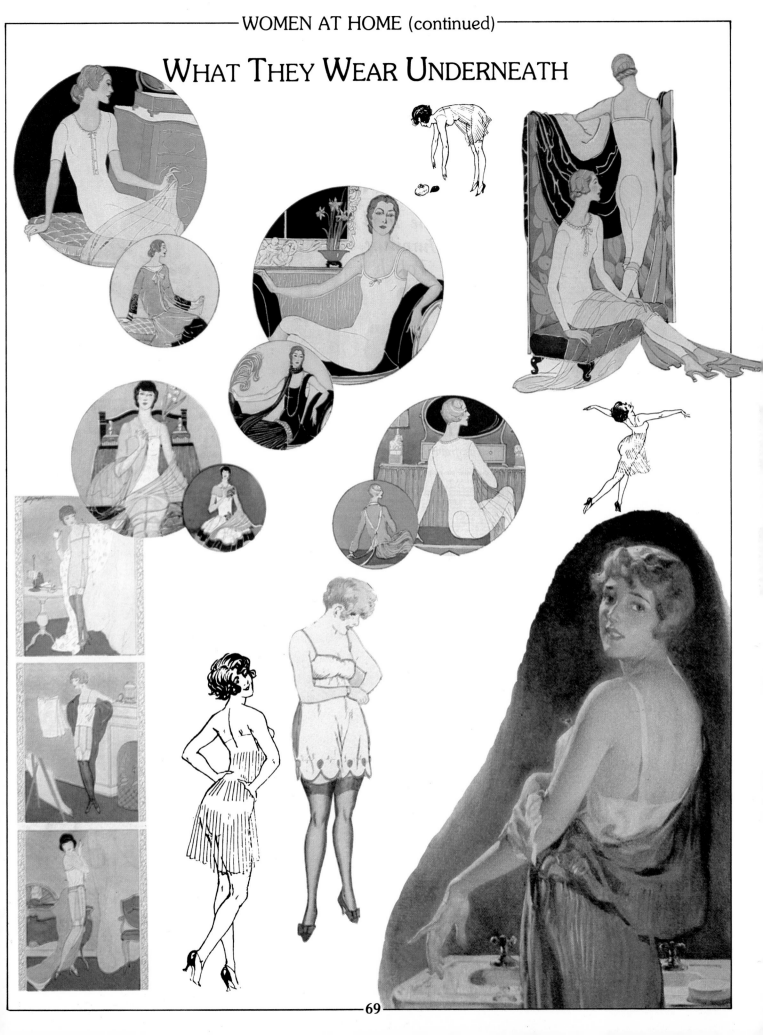

WHAT THEY WEAR UNDERNEATH

Underwear *for all the Family*

WHAT THEY WEAR UNDERNEATH

Nature gives women legs, to make men come running.

THEY PAINT IT ALL ON . . .

You can call a woman a kitten, but not a cat; a mouse, but not a rat, a vision, but not a sight. You can tell her time stands still when you gaze into her eyes – but you cannot tell her that her face would stop a clock.

For to nearly every woman, her face is her fortune (with a few exceptions – see "Women of the Town" page 32) and ever since the Egyptians, and earlier, women have painted, upon their face, another face – the one they would have preferred.

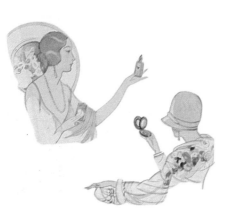

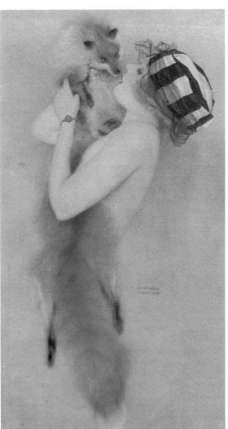

Beauty is only skin deep – and here are two beautiful skins.

My hair was a mess,
'Till I talked to young Bess
Who had prickly hair, like a pig;
But I've noticed of late
It's full-bodied, and straight
Since she washed it in
THINGUMMYJIG.

So I talked to young Di,
Whose hair was so dry
That it crackled and cracked like a twig;
Now it glows with a sheen
That is almost obscene,
Since she washed it in
THINGUMMYJIG.

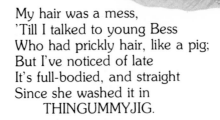

So I bought some from Boots, and I massaged my roots,
Just like they did, with
THINGUMMYJIG –
Now just look at mine! See it sparkle and shine!
Don't you think it looks fine? It's a wig.

AND THEY SCRUB IT ALL OFF

Cleanliness is next to Godliness, as the laundry-maid said when she put a crease in the Vicar's underpants. If this be true, then the ladies are the more virtuous sex, because they are, without doubt, much cleaner than men. How often, for example, do you see pictures of men getting in and out of the bath? About as often as you see pictures of the Loch Ness Monster.

Whereas the girls are to be seen leaping in and out of the water like dolphins, shoals of them; and I think I have provided a pretty good haul here.

Some pretty slippery customers, some of them, too.

All my family have been scrubbers,
and I'm a scrubber too.

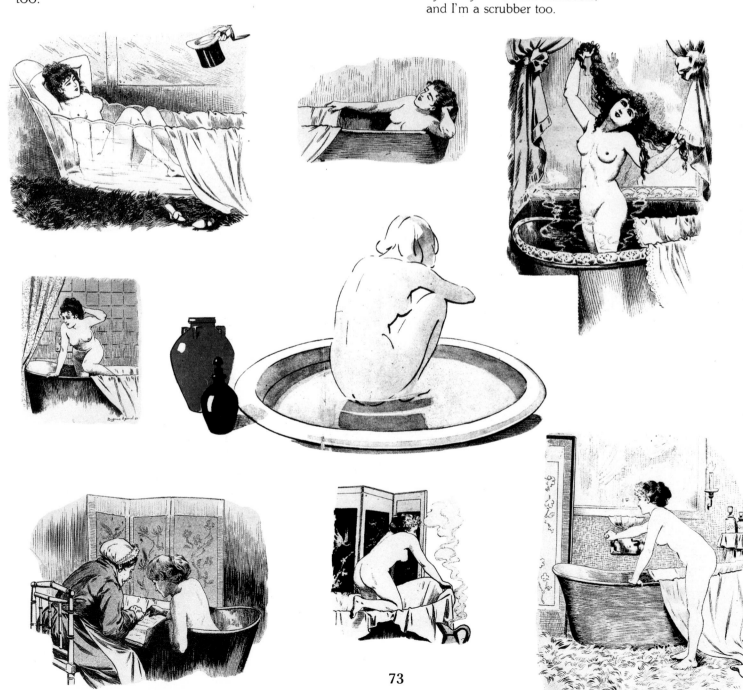

Here are some more ladies of the bath, from the pages of *La Vie Parisienne.*

Someone called Woman
the Thinking Rose –
Ah! But what does she think
about, do you suppose?

Diamonds

Others

Drama

NOTHING

One rose thinks only of the Dance,
Another thinks only of Love and Romance –
Another of Drama, of Thespia's call,
Another of Others, herself not at all –

Another thinks constantly, only, of *her*,
Another of Luxuries, Diamonds and Fur.
But I've got a girl not like any of those –
My non-thinking, sweet-smelling, beautiful Rose!

Herself

The Dance

AT ALL!

Romance

. . . and some postcards of World War One days, to show what the girls were (or were not) wearing in the Boudoir

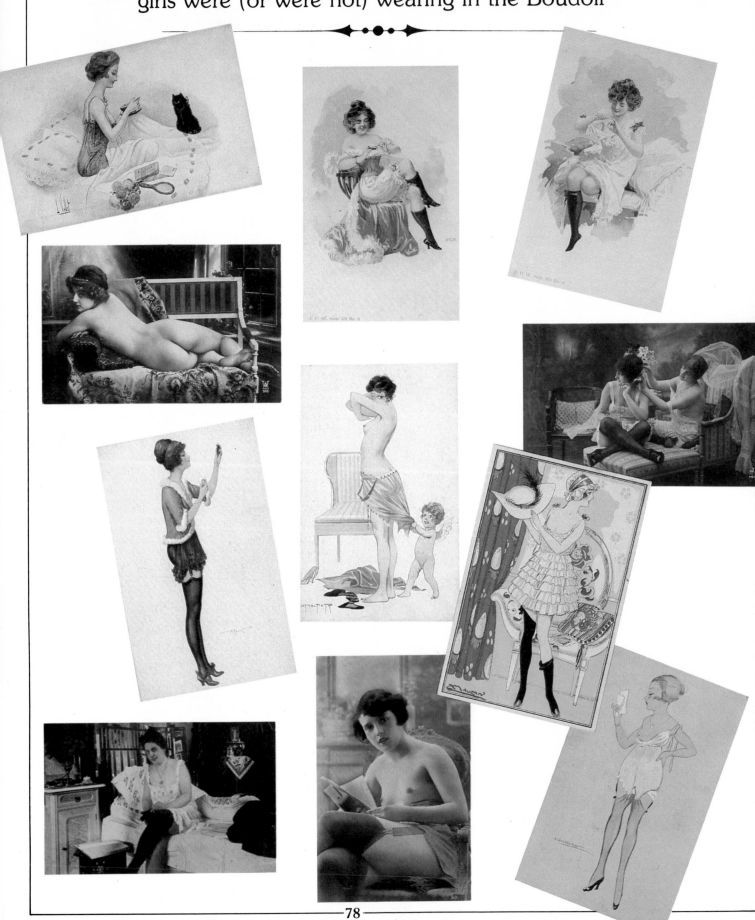

Mirror, Mirror, in my hand, who is the fairest in the
   land?
And if you say it's Muriel Mason, I'll smash your
   stupid-looking face in!

A stitch in time, they say, saves nine
I don't know if that's true,
By sewing up this dress of mine
At least I'm saving two.

Here three pretty girls you see,
Faith and Hope and Charity.
Faith first fell to Cupid's bow
At the Chelsea Flower Show.

Hope was abandoned first, they
   say,
On the sands at Whitley Bay.
But while her parents were at
   Frome,
Charity began at home.

A Day in the Life of (No 1)
An Artist's Model

1

A cold bath at
Six in the morning,
I'm off to the studio
by eight . . .

2

I pose as a serf for the artist,
And clean all his family plate.

3

I pose with a handful of lilies
I pose with a doll cavalier
I'm shouted at, bullied and badgered
I'm measured, and pinched in the rear –

4

I'm made to dress up like a soldier,
Made to crawl, crouch, cavort, lounge and lie –
Then when I get home to my boyfriend –
I have to pretend to be shy!

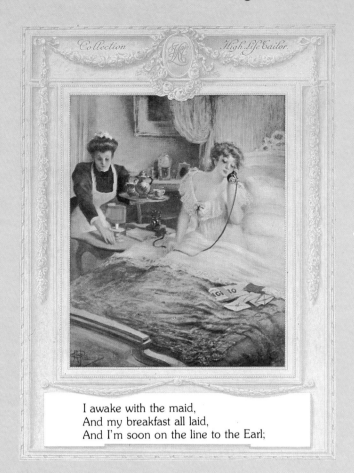

I awake with the maid,
And my breakfast all laid,
And I'm soon on the line to the Earl;

Then after a tub, and a rub and a scrub,
I emerge, a proud pink powdered girl.

On my mid-morning stroll,
Meet Le Duc de Chambrol,
Who is dying to make me his Duchesse;

Then Sir Algernon Doyle,
Who's a painter in oil,
With whom I've had several brushes.

A Society Lady

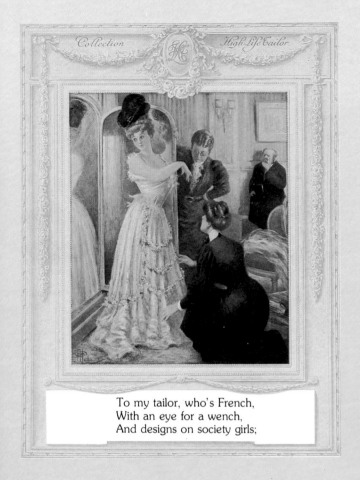

To my tailor, who's French,
With an eye for a wench,
And designs on society girls;

Meet Lord Charlesworthy for tea,
With his hand on my knee,
And his eye on my coconut whirls.

Then I dine with the count,
Who drinks quite an amount,
And is twenty-first heir to the throne —

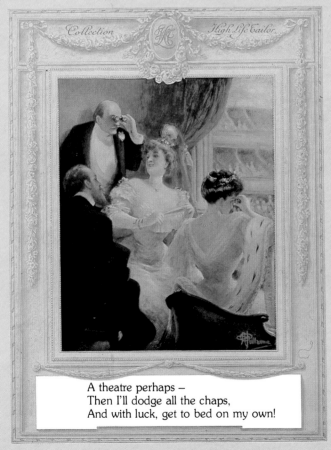

A theatre perhaps —
Then I'll dodge all the chaps,
And with luck, get to bed on my own!

A Day in the Life of No 3

A Greek God

9 A.M. Bathed the kids, dried them in front of the fire. Young Eros shot me in the foot with that flaming bow and arrow that Auntie Psyche bought him.

8 A.M. Woke up, to find Diana already out of bed, with the kids hanging round her as usual. Feel a bit jaded.

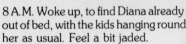

10 A.M. Went to the office, did a few letters. At coffee time that new typist started showing out a bit. Mustn't get too involved there, I might get to like it. Left about 12.30.

1 P.M. Home for lunch. It was chicken.

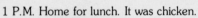

2. 30 P.M. Went shopping with Diana, called in at the Antique Market they have on a Friday. Bought an ornament for the spare bedroom (see detail above). I'm sure it's reproduction.

4 P.M. Got home, decided to go to the beach. Diana went in, I didn't bother. I keep slipping off the damn horses. Very crowded – couldn't move for kids.

6.30 P.M. Before dinner, Diana showed me the number she's doing in the Drama Club's musical evening. She is certainly an all-round performer. Sings and dances well, too.

8.30 P.M. Had a barbecue in the garden. Jason and Helen came round, and Juno. Also young Mercury, who got quite a lot of attention from Diana. I think she fancies him.

11 P.M. As usual, finished up a bit worse for wear. Diana passed out across Mercury's lap, but I was past caring. That new Beaujolais certainly takes you by surprise.

11.30 P.M. Got to bed, and dreamed about those three barmaids down at the "Golden Fleece". I must be getting old.

WOMEN IN LOVE

ould you ruffle the down of a butterfly?
Or scatter the violet's dew?
Would you rub the soft cheek of the peach
    awry?
Or rumple the roses? Would you?

And the first loving kiss of an unkissed maid
The fairest bloom ever that blew,
As sweet and as frail as the flowers that fade
Whoever would take it? Would you?

Well, of course, many people would, like a
shot. And who would blame them? (Beside
the father, of course, and he can get pretty
shirty if he wants to.) Because, to be honest,
women are the best

opposite sex we have, and all is fair in love and war, as the colonel said
when he kissed his second lieutenant.

    If you detect a rather heady, not to say hysterical, tone in these
garbled utterances, it is because love does tend to have this effect, be
it on king or commoner, prince or pensioner, duke, dustman,
debt-collector, or Deidre at the Post Office. All the world loves a lover
— and some of these I know you're going to adore.

Two of the oldest games in the world.

WOMEN IN LOVE (continued)

BOWLED OVER
Men, men, in rows of ten,
They'll fall, who e'er they be
I'll have them all, or none at all,
They all will fall for me!

He: Will you marry me?
She: No, but I will always admire your taste.

She: This is my father, Willie – you remember, I told
   you he's the one who takes things apart when they
   don't go.
He: Oh, y-yes!
She: So you'd better go now, Willie.

Outraged Husband: Saints alive – my own
   manservant!
Wife: But he loves me terribly.
Outraged Husband: Everything he does, he does
   terribly!

LOVE-SICKNESS: (In Love, and sick of it)

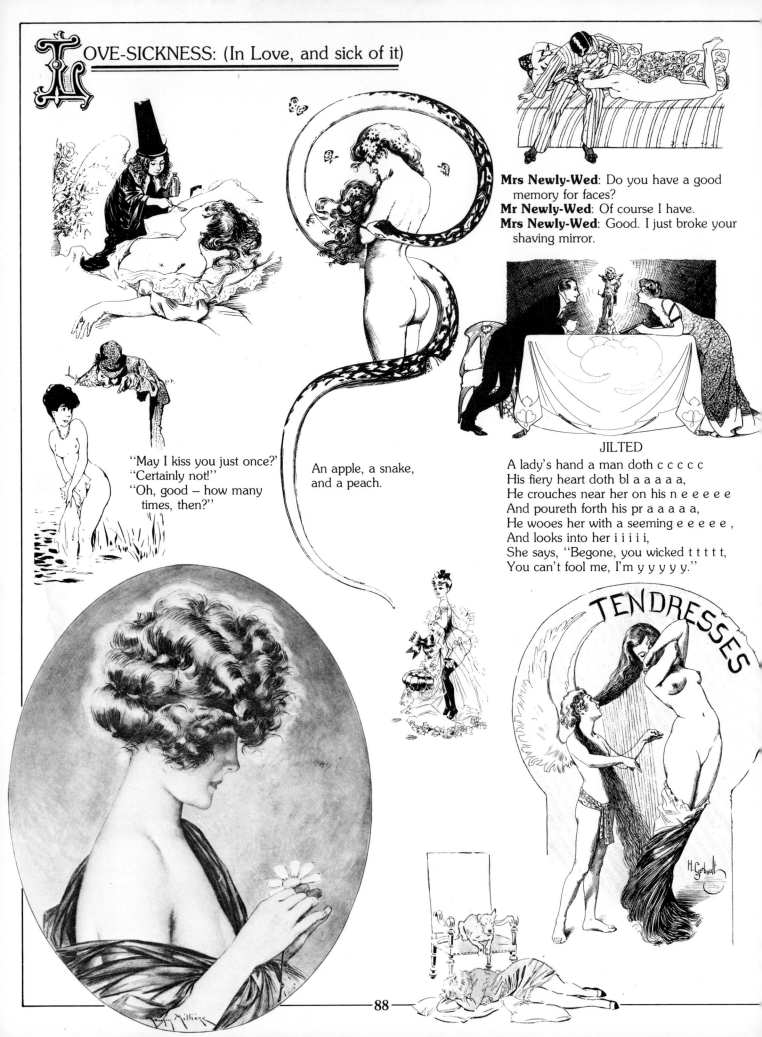

Mrs Newly-Wed: Do you have a good memory for faces?
Mr Newly-Wed: Of course I have.
Mrs Newly-Wed: Good. I just broke your shaving mirror.

"May I kiss you just once?"
"Certainly not!"
"Oh, good – how many times, then?"

An apple, a snake, and a peach.

JILTED

A lady's hand a man doth c c c c c
His fiery heart doth bl a a a a a,
He crouches near her on his n e e e e e
And poureth forth his pr a a a a a,
He wooes her with a seeming e e e e e,
And looks into her i i i i i,
She says, "Begone, you wicked t t t t t,
You can't fool me, I'm y y y y y."

TENDRESSES

He: I wonder if I could make you melt in my arms?
She: No – I'm not that soft, and you're not that hot.

Eve (to Adam): Are you sure I'm the first girl you've ever loved?

"The Milkman? Not today, thank you!"

A Quoi revent les jeunes filles

One handsome man, two girls, two hearts
Both pinned and pierced by Cupid's darts,
Should the wife be glad, and the lover sad?
No, the wife is sad, for the man's a cad
And the lover's the wife of another lad,
And that's where the trouble starts!

She: Every time I'm kissed it upsets my nerves. If you were a doctor, what would you give me?
He: A nervous breakdown.

"NO, MINE WERE SILVER."

He: Yes, my darling, I'd climb Mount Everest for you
  – I would walk on hot coals for you. I would
  endure any hardship for you.
She: Oh, darling! When will I see you again?
He: I'll pick you up on Saturday, if it doesn't rain.

SHE KNEW WHAT SHE WAS DOING.

If a man is too shy, then girlish mopes
Is no way to raise up the poor fellow's hopes,
Cinderella certainly knew the ropes.
  You really couldn't trip her.
When the prince was slow to make advance
And she fled in haste from the royal dance,
You don't really think it was by chance
  She lost the silver slipper?

"Late hours, they say, are bad for one,
Most people know that's true."
"Yes, darling, they are bad for one,
But awfully nice for two."

He: Darling, you're the kind of girl I'd like to take home
  to Mother.
She: Well, why don't you?
He: I can't trust Father.

The bride who said she would take her husband for better or worse – but not necessarily for good.

She: Well, darling boy, now you've made two people very happy – me and Mother.

Another mission accomplished.

He: Darling – tonight, will I be the first man ever to make love to you?
She: Of course. Why do all you men ask the same silly question?

1st Bridesmaid: Who's giving the bride away?
2nd Bridesmaid: I could, Angela, but I've promised to keep my mouth shut.

The Twopenny Dreadful

After marriage, much of the original pre-nuptial romance was recaptured
with the aid of these novelettes, avidly devoured by ladies of all classes.
The story below could *almost* have come from one of them.

BORN INTO RICHES

She drew a deep breath, followed by another. "I
think I'm being followed by another," she said.
They were standing in the sitting-rooom, near the
big window that overlooked the lawn. She could
see the distant figure of the gardener, who had also
overlooked the lawn for several weeks now. She
stared out, running her hands over her body
nervously. It was in terrible shape. All lumps and
bumps, with little tufts of moss growing in the more
inaccessible places.

"Followed? By a man?"

He felt something stir in his breast. It was the
tea-spoon in his waistcoat pocket, stolen from the
tea-shoppe that very afternoon.

"I think you're imagining things, darling."

"No I'm not."

He felt her quiver. "I've asked you not to feel my
quiver," she said. Her eyes swept the ground.
Then they dusted the mantelpiece, and cleaned
out the grate.

"You're overwrought, my dearest."

He felt for her, deep down. "Please, for the last
time, will you take your hand away," she said.

He turned away, thrusting his hands deep into his
trouser pockets and juggling with his conscience. A
whole minute passed.

"Have you got a grip on yourself?" she asked.

He didn't reply, but stared into the garden, his jaw
set at a strange angle; the result of a skiing accident
some years before.

"I'm sorry, Geoffrey," she said.

She leant back, and the colour rose in her cheeks.
She realised she was leaning against a hot radiator.
She sat down to cover her embarrassment; and
the cooling stone of the old window-seat through
her thin silk dress reminded her of her childhood. It
also reminded her that she had dressed

in a hurry, and had forgotten to put any on. The thought of sitting there, with him, in such a state of undress took her breath away. She took some brief pants before she dared speak, trying to slip them on without him noticing – but at the vital moment, he turned and caught her unawares – fortunately only with his elbow. He felt her quiver again as he took her in his arms; he couldn't resist it.

"I love you, Euphrosnia," he said, and those three simple words and one difficult one, sent a shiver through her cold frame. So much so that two of the cucumbers dropped off. He cupped her face in his hands, adding milk and sugar, before placing it to his lips, and planting a long hard kiss on her long hard nose. "It's been a long struggle to win you," he said, looking long and hard at her . . .

They were in the library, drinking in the beauty of the setting sun. "Have another," he murmured, indicating his cocktail shaker. She nodded. "Your hair is so beautiful," he said. Caught in the sun, it was a mass of tiny lights. She had got them off the Christmas tree last year. "How do you keep it so radiant?" She guided his hand to where she hid the battery. He touched it gently, and his eyes lit up. He raised his glass, and drawing her nearer to the fire, toasted her silently. She drained her glass at a single gulp. After a second, she spoke. After a fourth, she could hardly speak, and after a sixth, she was absolutely pie-eyed. He picked her up, and carried her on to the lawn, where the evening mist lay in a wispy grey swirl, and the gardener lay in a filthy blue shirt.

93

Geoffrey laid Euphrosnia on the lawn, watched by the old gardener. "That's the way, Sir!" he cried drunkenly. "All the best properties are mostly laid to lawn." As Geoffrey stared at the bumpy uneven surface, he realised that Euphrosnia's dress had ridden up, and so had a young lad on a bicycle.

"Doctor, your wife wants you. The old cow's about to give birth." The boy turned and cycled off again.

"Who'd be a vet?" thought Geoffrey, watching the boy getting smaller and smaller, until he was a tiny figure on the horizon. He eventually got so small he got a job in a circus, touring round as the Modern Tom Thumb.

Geoffrey gave one last look round at the vast, imposing edifice that was Euphrosnia's seat, and sighed.

"All this could have been mine," he said.

She lay, face downward, on the damp grass. The gardener, feeling the seeds of a strange turbulence growing inside him, removed a packet of radishes from his back pocket.

"Cheer up. Think how lucky you are. This is your seat," he cried, slapping her roundly; or, at least, one of her roundlies. "You're in Burke's Peerage. I've been looking up your particulars."

He, too, felt her quiver. "You men are all the same," she murmured. She breathed several sighs – first, a few small-size sighs, followed by several sighs of a much larger size. Finally, she drew him down on the ground beside her, with a felt-tip pen: the very pen that has since told this little story. Remember, of course, it isn't a true story; and, being only words, should not be taken literally.

The Type-setters Stop-gap

In these novelettes, it was customary always to include a "filler" story, or poem, which got pushed around from one page to another, throughout the magazine, wherever there was a space to fill.

Here is such a poem . . .

2 Oh Mary, Mary, hear my song
Come walk the woods with me
And I'll plant kisses all along
(Continued on page 3)

1 Oh Mary, meet me by the gate
I swear my love be true
And fain would tell you of my great
(Continued on page 2)

3 Oh Mary, Mary, say you'll be
Within my arms once more
And I'll again caress your warm
(Continued on page 4)

4 If only you will stay with me
Beyond the beaten track
I know our love-affair will be
(Concluded on the back)

95

GIRLS AT
CHRISTMAS

Christmas — the time when a wife turns to her overweight husband and says, "You won't need a pillow this year to play Santa Claus"; the time when she goes to cocktail parties and meets people who are so drunk she can't remember their names. The time for eating, drinking, and being merry; the time for doing all the things you want to do before those dreadful New Year resolutions start.

Time, too, for snow, slush, showers, sleet, slipping and sliding, and all the other inconveniences beginning with S.

The rich man's lot — the poor man's dream
To warm his Christmas heart:
A blazing fire, a good red wine,
A turkey, and a tart.

She: Yes, darling, but what else do you want for Christmas?

SNOW QUEEN

She bravely smiles as she flies the skies
The skies which the snow lies under;
But the North Wind blows, and she's got no clothes,
Snow Queen —
Snow fun —
Snow Wonder!

Some Christmas Games, as played in Victorian times:

A few Christmas stockings.

1 Postman's Knock
(Through the letterbox)

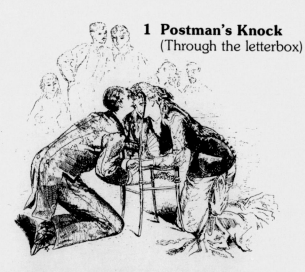

He: I hope that's what I'm sure I think it is — is it?
She: I think so. I'm not sure.

2 Sailor's Knock
(Through the porthole)

3 Chinese Knock
(Kissing sideways, knockers backwards)

4 Show-Jumper's Knock
(Three faults for a refusal, and a jump-off to decide the winner)

97

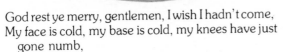

The tall one: What is the most Christmassy bird, Jane?
The small one: Dunno.
The tall one: I think it's the robin. It's on all the cards.
The small one: Yes. But turkey's on all the plates.

Look out, look out, Jack Frost's about, he's after
    your fingers and toes –
Whoever you are, be you skinny or stout, you'll
    freeze in the winter snows;
The snowman's got his paintbrush out, and the girl's
    got a cherry-red nose,
But the coldest things, without a doubt, are her cold
    little these and those.

God rest ye merry, gentlemen, I wish I hadn't come,
My face is cold, my base is cold, my knees have just
    gone numb,
If I stand here much longer I'll get frostbite in my
    thumb
And it's tidings of brandy and rum, brandy and rum,
And it's tidings of warmth inside my tum.

A stocking-filler.

The office party finished at ten,
And I've managed to dodge all the drunken men,
That new boy's asked if I'll see him again,
And he's touched my heart, I swear.
I suppose I should've been more aware,
At the office party you try not to care,
You expect to get touched almost everywhere –
But why did he touch me *there*?

The first little bud of the new season.

GIRLS ON ICE

A couple of pages to melt the most
frozen of hearts: the lady on the left
would certainly be skating on very thin
ice nowadays . . .

A curious custom was Norma's –
She'd skate without bloomers or
     warmers.
She kept frostbite at bay
By brandy, they say,
And slaps from the other
     performers.

Here comes Myrtle,
   there goes Myrtle –
See her hurry, watch
   her hurtle,
I can guarantee her
   skirt'll
Trip her up, and she'll
   turn turtle.

Après – Skate.

Oh, to cut a graceful skate!
Swishing and dashing a figure of eight
Stopping and starting and turning at will
Suddenly standing completely still;
Smiling and bowing to ladies who stare,
Breathing deep in the crisp winter air
Or pausing to offer polite advice
Then off again in a splutter of ice!

I slip and stumble and crash and curse
And my friend Brown is even worse;
But I'm quite content, and so is Brown
Sitting and watching the girls fall down.

A novel idea if your pipes burst.
Turn off the heating, open the
windows, phone your friends, and
make the most of the long winter
evenings.

1 Nothing to it.

2 Cold Comfort . . .

3 Three-point landing.

I find it warmer to
read about it.

POPULAR CHRISTMAS PRESENTS (No 1)
TIES and (Cigars)

A PLEA

Some men long for the soothing touch
Of lavender, cream, or mauve,
But the ties I wear must possess the
   glare
Of a red-hot kitchen stove.
The books I read, and the life I lead
Are sensible, sane, and mild;
I wear quiet gloves, I wear calm hats,
But I want my neckties wild.
Give me a wild tie, Dulcie,
One with a cosmic urge,
A tie that will swear, and rip and tear,
When it sees my old blue serge.

Some folks say that a man's cravat
Should only be seen, not heard;
But I WANT a tie that will make men cry
And render their vision blurred.
I yearn, I long, for a tie so strong
It will take two men to tie it,
If such there be, show it to me —
Whatever the price, I'll buy it.
Give me ties of enormous size
And a shire-horse team to pull 'em,
Ties that will blaze in a hectic haze
As the sun goes down over Fulham.

A WARNING

Beware, beware of the Christmas tie
That generous womankind love to buy,
It grips the throat with a strangle-hold
Its colours are crimson and green and
   gold,
It shameth the wearer with shame
   untold
Until he would wish to die.

Beware, beware of the gift cigar
Compounded of Cabbage-Leaf, Rope
   and Tar!
It fumes with the odour of burning hair;
It fills every bosom with Dark Despair;
Its cost is the half of a Tramway Fare —
And then it is over Par.

POPULAR CHRISTMAS PRESENTS

❧ No 2 ❧

FURS

When you hang a fur coat on the Christmas tree
The lady's delighted to find it.
For to her, it isn't the gift that counts,
It's really the price behind it.

She's grateful, and she tells you so —
You're broke, but you don't mind it.
For *you* know it isn't the gift that counts
But the wicked thought behind it.

And now, before we rejoin the ladies.

A FEW STORIES
(to be told to the ladies later)

A drunken voice had been phoning the switchboard operator for over an hour, at five-minute intervals, asking what time the bar opened in the hotel.

She repeatedly told him "Eleven-thirty", but still he kept ringing. Eventually she told the manager, and he lay in wait for the next call.

"Hello – what time does the bar open?" came the drunken voice.

The manager was curt. "We keep telling you, eleven-thirty, Sir. But I warn you, I shall be there personally to see you don't get in."

"I don't want to get in," said the voice, "I want to get out."

Jock had had one over the eight one lunchtime, and was staggering home, when he passed a house that looked vaguely familiar. He stared at it, and realised, after a minute or two, that it was his own, or at least he thought it was. He knocked the doorbell, and rang the knocker, which seemed to have no effect whatsoever. So he lay down on the steps to think it out, and the next thing he knew a pair of female legs were standing beside him. These, too, he seemed to recognise. He addressed them.

"Does Mr McCloud live here?" he mumbled.

The maid, for such it was, said: "You're Mr McCloud, Sir."

McCloud nodded. "I know, but do I live here?"

"Come inside Sir. I can see you're rather the worse for wear," said she.

"You're not supposed to be looking," said he, adjusting his kilt, "and mind your own business, girl!"

"Your old Uncle Willie has passed away while you were out, and the Undertaker has just been and laid him in his coffin. Shall I take you to see him, Sir?"

"I think you'd better, girl – I'll no make it on my own."

A few minutes later, Jock lurched into the front parlour, where the baby grand piano stood silent. He stared at it, tears welling up in his eyes.

"My, that's a beautiful coffin," he said. Peering even closer at the keyboard, he added, "And I'll say this for old Uncle Willie. He certainly took good care of his teeth!"

The large comfortable-looking woman sat down heavily next to a small, mild-looking fellow on the bus.

"Why, Johnny! After all these years!"

Johnny, who was stone deaf, nodded, smiling vaguely at her.

"Don't you remember me, Johnny? I used to nurse you, when you were a little 'un. And to think! Many's the time I've had you across my knee and given you a spanking! And now you're a man!"

Johnny thought he'd better pretend to have heard her. "Yes," he nodded, "you wouldn't know the old place now."

— PAYMENT ENOUGH —

The company director was taking some annual leave, simply to get into his garden and sort it out, while the September weather was still warm and inviting. Wearing his oldest sweater and Wellington boots, he stood clipping a yew hedge in his front garden, when an attractive middle-aged woman stopped her car, and beckoned him over.

"Tell me, my man, what do you get for working here – I might be able to offer you more."

"I doubt it, Madam," he said. "The lady here doesn't give me money – but she lets me sleep with her."

— SUFFRAGE —

A suffrage meeting was drawing to a close. The speeches had all been made and the meeting was thrown open to questions by the audience.

Said the presiding officer: "Now is there any woman here who would like to ask a question? Don't hesitate to ask any question you'd like to: any question at all about any phase of the woman question."

For a few minutes there was silence.

Then a woman arose and asked: "May I ask any question at all?"

"Certainly," said the speaker persuasively. "What question would you like to ask?"

"Well," said the woman, "I'd like to know how you got that smooth effect over your hips."

women On wheels

The woman behind the man behind the wheel has long been the subject of music-hall jokes. "Can you drive with one hand, Johnny?" "Of course, darling." "I thought so – here's an apple."

The other standard joke is the comparison of the parts of the motor-car with a girl's anatomy.

The words and pictures below are taken from advertisements of the twenties – presumably before the existence of such jokes, but they nevertheless make quite funny reading when applied to women . . .

"Bonnet and outer cladding easily removed for access to moving parts . . . . . . trim round rear . . ."

". . . concealed running boards, low hung doors, embossed panelling, and belled horizontal louvres . . ."

"Quality . . . you can feel it . . .

"Performance, plus
appearance, gives
satisfaction . . ."

"Ask the man who
OWNS ONE!"

"Seat-cushion and seat-back construction is the
result of years of research. It is the most durable,
and at the same time the most comfortable . . ."

"You will particularly like the stream-
line effect of the body, the placing of
the gas tank, and the generous com-
partment under rear deck . . ."

WOMEN ON WHEELS (continued)

Hire purchase firms with monthly terms
Are awfully nice to start with
But unless you pay, they take it away
(And it's dreadfully hard to part with).
They took my car, they took my clothes,
Which stops me going to parties
Now all I've got is a rather cold bot,
One wheel and a bag of Smarties.

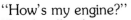

"How's my engine?"
"Looks all right to me, Miss."
"What's that knocking, then?"
"My knees, Miss."

It's the only way to travel.

He: Am I the first lieutenant
you've been engaged to?
She: Are you a first or a second
lieutenant?
He: I'm a first.
She: Then you're the second.

She: Could you see me across the
street?
He: I could see you a mile away.

"My motoring parties certainly bring people together, don't they, Mr Perkins?"

He: I hear your husband is in hospital. Was it an accident?
She: Sort of – I caught him with a blonde.

WOMEN
ON WHEELS
(continued)

"Remarkable acceleration . . ."

"Fourteen body types . . . two chassis
lengths . . . air-cooled throughout."

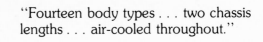

"Tough body, giving years of wear . . . adjustable
pneumatic seat for a comfy ride . . ."

She: If it has broken down, why don't we take a taxi?
He: I don't like taxis. If I sit with my back to the driver
I feel sick, and if I sit facing the meter I feel worse.

I brought them out
for a spin today,
Now, was I wise
to do it?
Whatever they get up to here,
They'll say I drove them to it!

WOMEN
ON WHEELS
(continued)

At the turn of the
century, women on bicycles
were even more vulnerable
to jokes and jibes – mainly
because of the more revealing, and often
comical costumes designed for the purpose.

Here are a few . . .

"When the girls sat in front
On the tandem,
Men's hands were completely
At random;
When their fingers got bold
By the girls they were told
To unhand 'em –
(We quite understand 'em)."

This way you don't
get saddle-sore.

The proud
one . . .

And the fallen.

A few more cycling oddities . . .

"Did you ever see me before?"
"No."
"Then how do you know it's me?"

Wood-nymph: "I'll make sure it's a nice day for it, anyway."

113

Riding for a fall.

GIRLS ON STAGE

The fatal fascination of the painted hussies who parade their charms within the footlights' glare is so universal it needs no words from me. Being, for want of a better term, a "theatrical" myself, I have worked with many, and have nothing but the most unstintng praise for every one of them. The girls of the chorus are a wonderful, lively bunch in a dreadful, dead-end job. I don't know why they do it. But I thank the gods they do: and those up in the "Gods" would be the first to agree with me.

She: Last night I went out with a man who completely turned my head.
He: Was he a gigolo?
She: No, a wrestler.

He: Hey, you. You ought to be able to sing.
She: Why?
He: You've got legs like a canary.

Voice from the "Gods":
    Drop dead!!
Madame Brigita: I'm sorry, I don't do requests.

"At the theatre last night, all of a sudden everybody got up and walked out."
"Good grief what happened?"
"the show had finished."

The party last night was a
  bore, dahling!
I go to so many of those;
The reason I stayed so
  long, dahling?
I couldn't find my clothes!

He: "Do you like the dictionary I bought you?"
She: "It's very interesting. Only it's hard to read,
  because it keeps changing the subject."

"You've heard of people getting
pearls out of oysters? Well, I get
diamonds out of old nuts."

He: I'm a doctor – if you married me, you could be ill
  for nothing.
She: No – I'm going to marry a vicar. Then I can be
  good for nothing.

1st Fiddle (to second fiddle): – She couldn't carry a
tune if it had a handle. Last night she came on stage
and sang "Goodbye, my love" and everybody went.

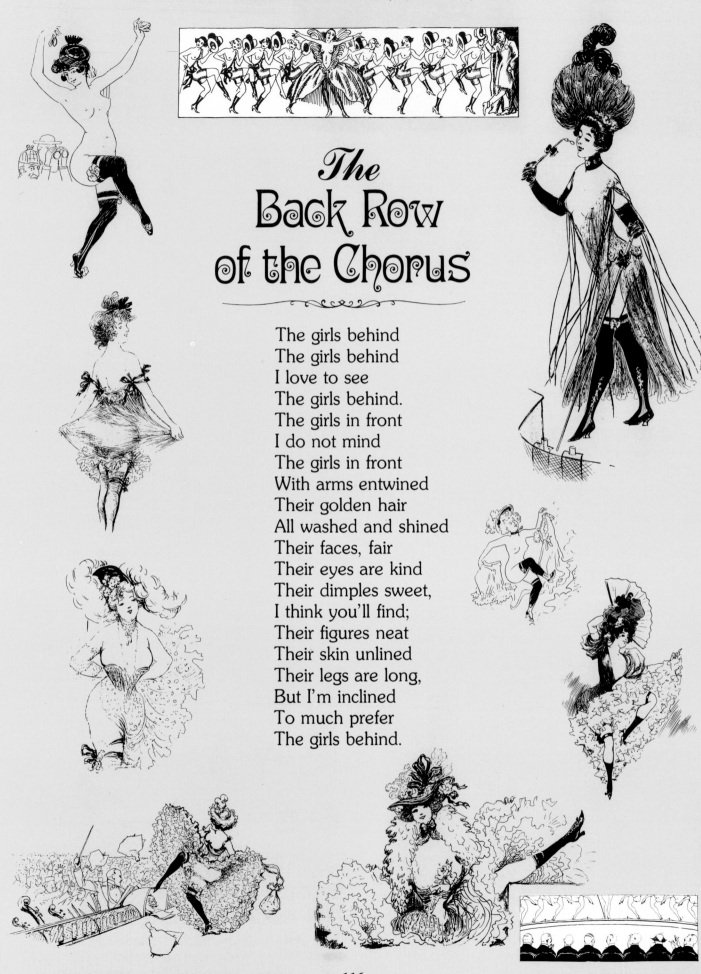

The Back Row of the Chorus

The girls behind
The girls behind
I love to see
The girls behind.
The girls in front
I do not mind
The girls in front
With arms entwined
Their golden hair
All washed and shined
Their faces, fair
Their eyes are kind
Their dimples sweet,
I think you'll find;
Their figures neat
Their skin unlined
Their legs are long,
But I'm inclined
To much prefer
The girls behind.

"I know it's a dress-rehearsal.
This is how I'm dressed."

The Girls in the Band

Some ladies playing musical things
Of every shape and size —